The bicycle has been called the world's happiest invention. I think I called it that. I dare anyone to argue. The bike is where joy and practicality meet, shake hands and head out for a ride. It's where adults kick their legs straight out, throw their heads back and coast along laughing and looking like freakishly large kids. It's where overprivileged overachievers push themselves to achieve even more. And it's where people with next to no means can take control of their forward motion. Blinged-out race ride or bare-bones transport, every bike is an honest machine for turning effort into motion. It can take care of itself, but it needs you to move. It's agile, quick to react, but steady. It can stand out among the crowd or blend, chameleon-like. It's the perfect companion. As loyal as a good dog and often longer-lived. (Though if I had my way, a good dog would live forever.)

The pages of this book are filled with people who see bicycles in many different ways. They see their bike as the joyful expression, the necessary tool, the personal statement, the next in a series of fun rides. It's an incredibly rich and varied mix. But however they see things, the bike love is evident in every portrait. The bikes are tended to. They're added to. They're looked up to. It inspires me, seeing all that love. I want to see more bike portraits, more bike love.

I want to see a big, beautiful country waking up to its big, beautiful bike potential. That's the kind of thing that gets me going. That's what it's all about.

Time to go ride.

Gary Fisher
The godfather of mountain biking

Bicycle Portraits

Neil Maling
Groot River, Haarlem, Western Cape, South Africa
2010/12/23 08:18

'I have a small farm in the Uniondale district. I'm very keen on cycling. It started when I was about nine years old. I went for my first bicycle trip and ever since then, me and cycling have been inseparable. The bike you see here I bought in 1985. What happened was, somebody said there was an organised bicycle tour in the UK from Land's End to John o' Groats and would I be interested? I went to a bicycle shop and they showed me this Peter Allan road bike, and I went on that tour to the UK. When I came back, I started going on cycling trips, taking my tent, cooking equipment and everything with me. And I decided I must get slightly heavier wheels so I got 27 by one and a quarter inch wheels that I use to ride very bad gravel roads… Let me tell you a story – we have always had very bad floods in this area, all over the Southern Cape. Once, all the bridges were washed away and nobody could get out by car, and there was a certain lady in my valley who desperately needed heart medicine. I was the first one who could get out of the valley because I could just take my bike and simply walk across the place where you could walk across the river, and cycle further. So I could get back across the river. Coming here into Haarlem, the river was overflowing too, so I waded through first to see if it wasn't too deep for me to walk across with my bike. And I found it was okay. So I waded over to the other side – I had taken my shoes off and I was about to put them on when a big lorry came through the river and made a big wave, and it took my cycling shoes and they went sailing down the river! I had to ride the rest of the trip barefoot! What I find fantastic about cycling is that you have a machine here which gives you a feeling of such absolute freedom. If you come to a locked gate, with a car you can't get over but with a bike you can just pick it up and push it over. You don't have to have a driver's licence, the bike doesn't have to be roadworthy. And I've also found that cycling around, people seem to just have such a fantastic attitude towards you. They're so friendly. You know, so often I'm cycling and they see this old bugger, going ahead on a bicycle that's packed high and they stop and they say, "Where in the hell are you going to and what are you going to do?"'

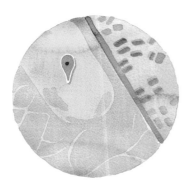

Edward September
Qomoyi Street, Nonzwakazi, De Aar, Northern Cape, South Africa
2010/07/29 15:13

'I'm off to go and sell this bicycle, as some of the parts don't work
any more and I don't have money to fix it. I'm going to the scrap yard.
They weigh it there, maybe they'll give me R12 or R11. I already took
the wheels. When the bicycle was working I used it every day – people
sent me to fetch things for them.'

Willem Johannes Willemse
Stockenström Street, Worcester, Western Cape, South Africa
2011/07/05 10:29

'Listen people, let me tell you, I've been riding this bicycle for almost 12 years. I built it up like this and it helps me wherever I go. Whatever my wife asks me to do, I do it with this bicycle. When we go shopping she sits on the front and we put the groceries on the back. This bike keeps me on the road – and my eyes are always on the road too, because there are cars in front of me and cars beside me. I ride it to the river with my fishing rods, and I pack everything on there – even the *potjie* that I cook my food in next to the water. When I get back home my wife has to cook the fish. And all the children sit down next to me at the table so we can eat our fish. On top of my bicycle here is a little stove for my wife, in which she can bake a cake, because 28 May is my birthday, when I'll turn 61! I'll ask her, *"Wat gaan jy maak vi' my?"* I'll say, *"Dankie my bokkie, ek's lief vi' you, man! Ek sal elke dag by you staan."*'

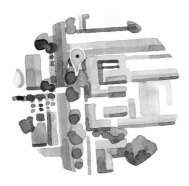

Mike Fortuin with Lucinda Kammies
Church Street, Prince Albert, Western Cape, South Africa
2010/04/27 12:53

'We're going to the municipality to buy electricity. Then we're going home. I can only ride in town. I'm not allowed to ride to school on my bike. My mom is scared someone will steal it…'

Brandon 'Doom' van Eeden
The promenade, North Beach, Durban, KwaZulu-Natal, South Africa
2011/03/15 22:20

'I ride because Durban has such a great promenade. I've seen pictures of cruisers on the beachfronts in California that look like they would suit our promenade as well. I started looking online for bicycles I could get locally, but came up blank for the style I was after, so I ended up importing one from 3G Bikes that I really liked. Gary da Silva has been making bikes his whole life (and his father before him) and is credited with bringing the retro-chopper trend to life. He named 3G Bikes in honour of the three Gs in bicycling: Gary Turner (GT Bikes), the godfather of BMX; Gary Fisher, credited with inventing mountain bikes; and Gary Klein, who is credited with much of the aluminium-welding technology used in bicycle manufacturing today. Because I live very close to work, I find traffic to be quite easy to negotiate. Motorists definitely aren't used to cyclists, though, so you have to pedal defensively at all times. Durban has the worst drivers in the country. My nickname, "Doom", comes from my ex-bandmates. I described certain sections of music we wrote as 'doomy', those were always the ones I really liked. Or maybe it's because I wear a lot of black lately? I've been vegetarian for over 15 years. It's just something that seems to come naturally to me. My main reason is that I disagree totally with how modern food production methods have made animals a product, an industry. Straight Edge is a subculture that started in the early '80s in the hardcore/punk music scene as reaction to the hedonism of the punk scene in those days. Instead of drinking and taking drugs, a small minority started shunning that lifestyle. Today it's a worldwide subculture of thousands of people who identify with the "clean living" philosophy and live these ideals to varying degrees. I just try and live life the way it makes me happiest. My bicycle feels like an extension of me, but perhaps even better – it's pure and simple, a machine of integrity.'

Afrika Waterboer
Church Street, Graaff-Reinet, Eastern Cape, South Africa
2010/12/10 13:28

'I'm 63. I've been riding this bike for more than 15 years. I bought it from my uncle. I actually just bought the frame, and I then bought the wheels and other things to get it right. I ride it every day to work and back home. I do gardening work. I worked for Koos Minnaar in his garden for 18 years. He passed away and since then I've been working for four or five years, one day here at this house, the next at another house. Here in the back I have something I bought for my house, the leather bag is for my food I brought this morning that I've already eaten and there's other stuff – bananas and so on. I got the saddle off my old bike that Koos Minnaar gave me before he died. But my kids rode that bike into a car and it buckled the front wheel so badly that I couldn't fix it. I took the saddle and put it on this one. At the moment I'm riding with just one brake – I'm not really fast, I ride very slowly. And the hooter I use if there is someone in the way… I use it a lot because people don't want to get out the way, especially for a bicycle! The light here on the front I also got from the bike that Koos Minnaar gave me, but it's not working at the moment.

But this bike means a lot to me – if I think about it, if I took the taxi everywhere, it would be R12 a day, and with the bike I just make sure the tyres and tubes are fine and then it costs me nothing. At night I lock it in a small outside room.'

Sibusiso Nsibande
Naudé Street, Ermelo, Mpumalanga, South Africa
2011/07/09 17:57

'I'm here to visit my brother in Wesselton. I use the bicycle when I want
to go a long distance – it helps you get where you want to go. It also
prevents us from getting robbed. When it is cold as well – it helps
when you are on a bicycle. When I go to work in the morning, I use it.
When people bother me about hurrying, then I get there fast. That's it.'

Peter Masilo
Ramohatla Road, Jericho, North West, South Africa
2010/05/30 15:57

'I use this bicycle every day. I do some work locally, building houses.
I've been using the bicycle for three years. It's good because I can
go to places – to Maboloka or Letlakane, and sometimes just to the
post office. I don't know many people who live here. I live here with
my mom: she is old, 66, and right now she is sleeping. I'm 48.'

Wouter Coetzer
Schoeman Street, Hofmeyr, Eastern Cape, South Africa
2010/12/13 18:29

'I'm a teacher here at the school – just around the corner – and my wife is a secretary. I usually walk to school and then cycle in the mornings or afternoons. You know I've always loved cycling because as a young boy I used to deliver the newspaper, *Die Burger*, while I was growing up in Die Hel. This is actually my son's bike. When he moved to Germany a few years ago I decided to start cycling again. We've been living here in Hofmeyr for about 25 years. At the moment here in town it is only me who cycles. Hofmeyr originated because of the crossroads – there are five or six roads that come together here. It's the Cradock main road, the Schoombee road, the Molteno road, the Queenstown road and the Middelburg road – they all cross here. This is also the shortest route from Port Elizabeth to Johannesburg. We have about 350 kids at the school, going up to Grade 9, and about 18 teachers, half white and half black. It is going very well and I can't complain. I enjoy teaching. I only teach Afrikaans. Currently we are reading *Die Dag Van Die Reuse*. It's a book about the border war in Mozambique, how everything is wiped out and one little boy survives.

But it is actually about the elephants. One elephant steps on a land mine, and then the boy takes care of it and nurses it. Then he leads all the elephants out on a path where there aren't any land mines. The rebel groups see this and salute him – in their eyes he's become a giant, because the elephants listen to him. I've ordered *Tin Tin* for next year.'

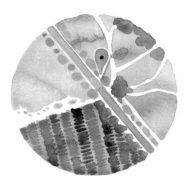

Inock Banda
Orpen Road, Tokai Forest Reserve, Cape Town, Western Cape, South Africa
2010/04/10 15:41

'I bought this bike one year ago. I like riding my bicycle. I'm Malawian,
and I came to South Africa in November 2008. I also had a bicycle
in Malawi. I like the exercise. But it's more dangerous here because
there are lots of cars. Malawi has much fewer cars than here. Luckily
since I came here I've had no accidents. I have a helmet but because
it's hot today I left it at home. I prefer this bike to a mountain bike
because this one rides very quickly, ha ha! But the tyres are finished.'

Gams Hassen
Carr Street, Kimberley, Northern Cape, South Africa
2010/08/06 12:17

'I do it for myself, I've got, like, a tuck shop. I bought the bicycle frame at a scrap yard, and then I came across this carrier. You see, you shouldn't make a bicycle beautiful, ha ha – you'll just make it pretty for another thief, ha ha. I ride a motorbike too – it stands there at home, 'cause just now it will make me old. It is good to keep oneself loose. I shouldn't sit around. I've been riding over 20, 30 years. I'm 55 now. I've got another two or three bicycles at home. I still ride those old-time ones – those with the carriers in the front. This bicycle has a mountain bike fork. The original fork was not that strong. I can ride down from the pavement, nothing happens. See, this bike is carrying a load. I don't ride there in the road. I just say, "Hey!" and ring the bell, I'm not going to bump you, just excuse me. These guys in the cars, I don't know them. They might be drunk or pills-drunk – look, our thoughts aren't running the same, I'm riding my way and he is riding his way. I used to work, making furniture and school desks. That was my last job. Look, the money the government gives us is only meant for rent, insurance and just a little bit of food, not a lot. I'm not working for anyone any more, I'll work for myself until I die. I do things like gather beer bottles. I give them 20 cents for a bottle, then I go and get 50 cents. That way the money increases a little, like a money box. Now where am I going to get money that easily?'

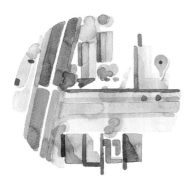

Walton Koetaan
College Street, Jansenville, Eastern Cape, South Africa
2010/12/09 18:10

'I've had this bike for about 13 or 14 years. I bought it at an auction for R2 000. I love it very, very much. Last year my son did the Cape Argus Pick n Pay Cycle Tour on it, and he was very impressed. This bike stays in the house, not in the garage – that's how serious I am about it. I haven't been riding so much lately, though, because the roads in our area are being destroyed by heavy ore-carrying trucks, and the R75 is so narrow that riding on it can be a danger to your life! My dream is to ride the 40-kilometre Somerset East-Pearston race – we call it the *Bruintjieshoogte* tour – next year…'

André Seupershad
Erskine Terrace, Durban, KwaZulu-Natal, South Africa
2011/03/13 18:02

'My name's André. My surname is Seupershad. Today I came to
see my brother, Adrian, here at Addington Hospital. He's in ward
10B. He's got an abscess in his lungs. We are waiting for visiting
hours to start again at 7pm so we can go see him. We came to
see him earlier, from 12pm to 2pm, and while we were waiting
I was just riding my bike along the shore. He is my twin brother.
And I have a sister. Her name is Nirvana. Me and my brother share
this bike. I miss him a lot. Recently I've been focusing more on him –
my studies and all, I know they come first, but he's the most important
one in my life. I don't know what I'd do without him. We are just busy
packing the bicycle in my father's car so we can go and see Adrian.
I take off both the wheels. That's why you can see one wheel is missing.'

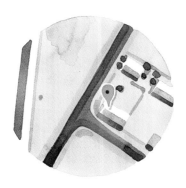

Pieter and **Lal Snel**
Wes Street, Kenhardt, Northern Cape, South Africa
2011/04/13 09:57

Pieter: 'My son, so long ago… We went to town to buy him some
shoes, but we couldn't find anything that he liked. He was in a hurry
to go home so I gave him my bicycle, and I started walking back.
When he got home he decided he wanted to bring my bicycle back
to me. I saw him coming up the road – he was so close. It was then
that the accident happened. Just there, at the crossing, where the
road curves. Right in front of me. The car's windscreen was completely
smashed. The ambulance came and they took him to hospital, but by
the time they got there he was dead. The police also arrived and put
the bicycle in the back of their van. On Monday morning they took
his body to Upington for an inquest.'
Lal: 'And that is why you should warn people…'
Pieter: 'This is why I never let children ride on my bicycle. I might
ride really slowly, but only I use it – and I don't ride on the tar roads
at all. When that accident happened, it taught me. I just don't feel
safe on the road. People drive too fast and too wild.'

Takura Chadoka with Mango Mogeni
Corner Hout Street and Burg Street, Cape Town, Western Cape, South Africa
2010/06/11 18:11

Takura: 'We came to Long Street where there are a lot of people, where
you can feel the vibe of the World Cup. I'm not a big soccer fan, you
know, but just to feel the vibe that's all around, that's cool! I don't really
care for soccer, but I like bicycles. If there was something for bicycles
I would go for bicycles. I have two bikes: this one and a small mountain
bike that I'm going to give to my niece. I'm thinking of building a fixie
bike – that's my next project, because I like fixed-gear…'
Mango: 'I like bicycles too, *ja*. I'm going to get a bicycle!'
Takura: 'You see this kid? I like him because he likes bicycles, you
know. He's always trying to ride this one, but it's too big for him. He
has a small bicycle but it's broken. That's why I'm taking him around
on the BMX. I'm going to try and fix his bike.'

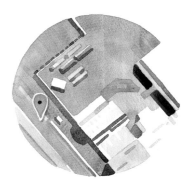

Rouan Robyn
Metrorail train en route to Kuilsrivier station, Cape Town, Western Cape, South Africa
2011/05/08 16:51

'Since I got this bike four years ago, I've ridden it every day from
where I live in Eersterivier to where I work in Kuilsrivier. I get on the
train with my bike every day – they used to charge me to take it but
now it's for free, I think. Maybe they just got used to me. Or got tired
of giving me hassles. Even though it's allowed now, I still get hassles
sometimes. I call my bike "Red Devil" – I can't tell you why, I just do.
I saw this frame lying at my *tjommie*'s house, so I asked him about it
and he said I could have it. I went to the local scrap yard, where they
have good bicycle parts, and I bought everything there to build it up.
It has been stolen twice but both times I got it back within a few hours.
People around here know my bike. If someone takes it, they will get it
and bring it back to me. My bike is almost like a car to me – but better.
It doesn't take much longer to get somewhere and I don't have to pay
for petrol. My girlfriend, Yvette, also prefers me to ride a bike: she says
a car just leads to the wrong kinds of friends and other girlfriends!
She knows – we're getting married in September…'

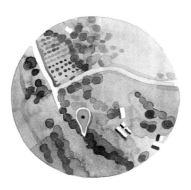

Wilhelmina Parsons
Jonkershoek Road, Stellenbosch, Western Cape, South Africa
2010/09/28 17:10

'I cycle to work every day. It is better than walking because the road
up here is really very long, ha ha! I've had this bicycle for a year now,
I didn't have one before. It was given to me by Lionel Johannes. It
gives me lots of problems – the tyre gets punctures and sometimes
the back wheel moves out of position. Here in my basket at the back
I have some wood and my jacket. The wood is for when we *braai*. I'm
heading home, it's still a long way, all the way to where the road stops.
There I live with my boyfriend … and his parents. He also cycles: he
has a racer bicycle, which doesn't break so much!'

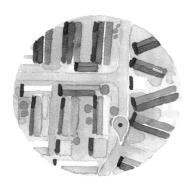

Donald Gxowa
Jungle Walk, Langa, Cape Town, Western Cape, South Africa
2010/01/14 16:42

'I've been riding bikes for over 16 years – and this one for more than
five years. I think I ride maybe five kilometres per day… I have just
come from the Maitland Post Office. I don't take this bicycle home
– it must stay at the Post Office. But even if I had my own bike at
home I wouldn't ride it. I'm tired, man!'

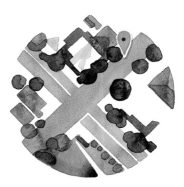

Barry Truter
Ferguson Road, Bulwer, Durban, KwaZulu-Natal, South Africa
2011/03/15 17:39

'I have an art studio here at the back where I do artworks, sculptures and prints. I'm a printmaker, so I do etching, lithography, silkscreening and wood etching, even stained-glass work. I've been cycling since 1984, often to the college where I teach, about 1,8 kilometres away. Years ago I had a motorbike but it was stolen, and it was then I bought the bicycle. Later I bought a road bike, so every morning I get up at 3am, have some coffee and around 3.30am I go for a ride for about 20 kilometres. Then I come home and get ready for work. It gives one an appetite you know, ha ha! I've been attacked a few times. Someone once chased me with a knife and I had to cycle away real fast. So now I take a knife or a truncheon with me in my backpack. I like going early because the air is fresh, if you wait until 5am then all the cars pollute and people come out. Unfortunately I have to go to bed at 8pm. Sometimes I take the delivery bike to work, also to go shopping; loading a bag of potatoes on the front, a bag of onions on the back and some vegetables on the handlebars – you know the brakes are backpedal so there is some space on the handlebars. There are very few people who cycle to work here in Durban, I've seen two or three. I've had this road bike for about 10 years. I like it because it still has a stamp from Italy and it is original. These days everything has nice paint and design but there's a bunch of crap underneath. Back in the day I paid R10 000 for this bike. These days they cost R25 000 or R30 000, and I don't really think they're better. The only thing that's changed is the amount of gears. But I don't know if you need all those gears if you are racing, you know. Just when you change gears you lose speed. If you keep on a high gear you can cycle fast – you just need to pedal, ha ha!'

Jeffrey Klaas
St Andrews Street, Bloemfontein, Free State, South Africa
2011/03/03 08:25

'For many long, long years I've ridden a bicycle. I use it for transport, for working, for going to my appointments – for everything I do. I like it very much. One day when I was riding a sports bicycle, a mountain sports one, I got in an accident: I crashed into a person. It became a long story as I was going too fast, so I ended up having to spend a lot of money to pay that guy. And the bicycle was messed up, so I had to pay money to fix it. It is a memory for me now. After that, the other story is that I don't have another story to tell. Only that I have changed from a mountain bike to a racer, and now I'm riding a BMX.'

Ernestus Segers
Grey Street, Phillipstown, Northern Cape, South Africa
2010/07/31 13:25

'I bought a piece of property just outside town, where you can keep about 20 sheep. As it is quite close I decided I will walk. But after a while I started thinking that walking wastes time and sometimes you got things to do – so I bought a bicycle. It's been about two years now. I cycle there in the morning, come home around 10am to eat and around 2pm I head back and then I *tjaila* around 5pm again. It's great exercise, you know. It is only about a kilometre to my property, but you'd be surprised as to what it does to a person, just the fresh air and the fact that one doesn't sit and rust up. Look, you know, life is a chase. With a bicycle you have an opportunity to look around you. I often cycle around town and have some usual places I stop at, spending time with people along the way. With a motorcar you are always heading somewhere in a hurry. I have a story to tell about a bicycle. Our deacon in Vrede – rich, with lots of property, farming about 3 000 sheep – came one morning to the *koöperasie*. He saw a group of guys standing around, talking and looking very unhappy. He asked what the matter was and they told him that the brand-new bicycle of one of the guys was stolen the night before. He sympathised with them, mentioning that someone had stolen 300 sheep from him the week before. They didn't sympathise with him, saying he had lots of sheep, but this guy only had one bicycle and it was the only thing he had!'

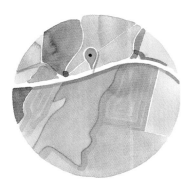

Peter John Heneke
N2, outside Heidelberg, Gauteng, South Africa
2011/07/17 17:25

'My father found this bicycle in Kensington. Apparently his aunt's children weren't interested in it any more, and it was just lying there, getting ruined. He found it there while he was on holiday, doing some little odd jobs at my aunt's house – so he asked if he could have the bicycle as payment for helping out there. She said it belonged to her eldest child but that they didn't ride it at all any more. That's how he ended up bringing it home. We checked it out to see what it would take to get it working properly. I bought parts for it and we got it rolling again. Initially we just rode it around the house – just for fun. But after a while I realised that I can use this bicycle for something else as well – I started riding it to work, to church and to go shopping. I started thinking that it doesn't look that attractive to me as a young man, so I decided to decorate it a bit. I got this white insulation tape – that is where my mags come from – and the yellow stripes to make me more visible as a road user. They've been making changes to this national road but they haven't made it easier to ride a bicycle along it. But we push through the dangers. This bike means so very much to me,

I'm very pleased with it and very proud of it – through thick and thin, through storms and quiet days… I would say if anyone wanted to buy this bike I would never sell it. You know, this is an imported frame, it's not a South African frame, it's originally from England. *Ja, dankie.*'

Andries Toring
Murray Street, Tarkastad, Eastern Cape, South Africa
2010/12/14 14:11

'*Joo!* I've been cycling for years, I grew up on a bicycle. Nowadays
I collect corrugated iron and metal, because there is a guy who buys
all this stuff here. I load it on the back, just for a little something extra
to buy electricity and tobacco. I went from my house to the dump,
loaded up and came here to unload all the metal scrap I found.
That's how we survive. I made this little trailer myself to help me
carry things. On the side here I've tied my "gun". It's my stick for
hitting people if they try and block me. I don't make trouble, but
you never know. At least I've never had to use it!'

Eben Jones
Bicycle lane through Metro Industrial Township, Cape Town, Western Cape, South Africa
2011/08/11 16:40

'Hello, I work in Paarden Island. I ride my bicycle every day – over this little bridge on my way home. For me it's a pleasure to ride a bicycle: it keeps me healthy and fit, and … how can I say … it's *lekker*. I really don't like taxis. The bicycle is faster and it's better for me. I've got another bicycle at home – my show bike, my Sunday bike, as they say. I put it away for a while because it was getting spoiled, the tyres were spoiled by all the stones and everything. Every Sunday I give it a polish. When you ride, the spokes have to shimmer in the light. It's like a car to me. But I'm happy to ride this mountain bike. I paid R250 for it. It was definitely worth the money…'

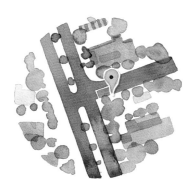

David Mamabolo
Lange Street, Nieuw Muckleneuk, Pretoria, Gauteng, South Africa
2010/04/08 17:27

'I've had this bike for about five years. Here in the front I've got some loading space for the clothes that I work in. I'm a gardener. I'm 60. I enjoy this bicycle very much and I use it to go to work. It is great, because I work in five different places. You know, many people ask me to sell this bicycle to them, but I always say no. You see it's an old one like me. I don't like the new bicycles. If this one is broken, I just visit the bicycle shop, buy the parts and fix it myself.'

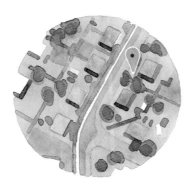

Martin 'Silky' Afrika
Loop Street, Noordend, Prince Albert, Western Cape, South Africa
2010/04/12 19:34

'Inspiration – you just have to let your mind go and your hands
do the work. My inspiration, that's what it's all about. If you have
no inspiration, you'll get nowhere in life. I thought far, and I thought
deep, and I tried, and I got it right. I've made two of these bicycles –
tall ones. I just took a frame and turned it around – it's not two bicycles
on top of each other – I turned it over and cut loose where I had to,
and attached tubes where I needed to, and that is how I made a tall
bicycle. I'm a guy who likes fun, and I like being funny. That's how
I am and that's how I'll stay. That's why I'm called "Silky" – I'm smooth.
But it's not just about the girls, I do have a wife! I'm just missing her
here next to me…'

Junior Stander
Lanyon Street, Amsterdam, Mpumalanga, South Africa
2011/07/09 11:39

'I was born in Bloemfontein in 1988, in the Universitas Hospital. Then we moved here… I got this bicycle from a guy who wanted to trade it for my motorbike. He wanted to build a go-kart out of it. I asked my dad if it was okay and he said yes. The guy brought me the bike and I figured out how the little motor works, and how to adjust the chain and all that stuff… It had a problem before: the chain used to slip off if you switched on the motor while you were riding. I lined it all up and tightened the chain, and from then on it's been riding smoothly. At the moment I don't have the two 12-volt batteries attached here in the back, they're being charged. I normally just strap them on with old tubes. So it's a front-wheel drive – when you switch on the motor it pulls with the front wheel. You must check it when the batteries are fully charged! You know, I "drift" with the bike, or I wheelie, or I ramp, or I do a "stoppie". My *tjommies* and I found a big *stoep* outside the municipality offices that's very smooth. We used to pour water all over it and do doughnuts and "burnouts", but now they closed it off with a railing… We're not allowed to ride there any more.'

LECA split into two factions

Riding out of Maseru, the border town on the edge of Lesotho and South Africa, and through the Maluti Mountains is like being on top of the sky. I love that on a bike you get to see the world in a new way. That's just one of the ways cycling has changed my life…

While other children in my village of Khubetsoana were buying sweets with their pocket money, I was renting bicycles. From the little I earned helping my mother sell crafts to tourists near the border, I'd rent bikes from a man in my village. R6 got you an hour on one of his old BMXs.

I became friends with a train mechanic who passed through the border a lot and thanks to him I got my own bike – a BMX from Johannesburg. Owning it was like winning the lottery. It was like a car to me and my life became a little bit easier. I could get to wherever I needed on my own steam: 4 kilometres to my school or 200 kilometres to visit relatives in the mountains. I rode every day, everywhere – after school during the week and longer distances on weekends. The training would be useful later.

Then in 2002 at the age of 20, I took part in the Tour de Lesotho – my first professional race, competing with cyclists from all over the world. I'd added road-bike parts to my BMX to make it go faster, but I knew

the international cyclists were looking at my bike and thinking, 'No way he's going to make it.' It was an 86-kilometre ride – the uphill was 2 286 metres long. But I completed the race in four hours and 47 minutes – better than a lot of the top athletes. I finished my second race in four hours and 40 minutes, the third in four hours and 36 minutes. Slowly, I was getting better.

Cycling in Lesotho is like nowhere else in the world – there are a lot of challenges, but you must learn to overcome them. Like, once, in the middle of my first race with a real mountain bike, my gear cable snapped. No problem. I picked up a stone and shoved it in the rear derailleur, aligning it to an easier gear, and rode in one gear all the way to the finish line. I finished in three hours and 52 minutes.

In 2006 I represented Lesotho at the Commonwealth Games in Australia. The Queen's Baton Relay traditionally takes place before the Games begin. The baton went to all 71 countries of the Commonwealth. I was selected to hold it in Lesotho and I built a golden bicycle especially for it. Competition in Melbourne was tough, but I came first in my country. Waking up at 3am to train suddenly seemed worthwhile!

Holding the Queen's Baton was a very proud moment for me, but my favourite thing about cycling is not winning medals or holding batons – it's being able to change people's lives like mine has been changed. There are a lot of youngsters in my village drinking, smoking, fighting, insulting each other. Unemployment is high, most of the adults drink beer all the time – and the children learn from them. So I've decided to use cycling to better the lives of others – to empower the Basotho youth and instil in them a love for the sport. Cycling keeps you fit and healthy, and it saves money, because you don't have to pay for transport.

So I started a nonprofit project – Tumi's Bicycling Club – and opened a workshop so I can repair bicycles. (Many are made out of car parts, whatever's lying around.) I help the youth with training and organise races to highlight issues such as HIV/Aids. It's a big motivation – cycling offers an alternative to drinking and drugs. I want to show them there is another way to live. I want to make their parents proud.

Recently I took 10 bikes that had been donated to me to a group of young people in my village. I said, 'If I hear someone insulting someone else, I won't let you ride.' They've changed – now they are medal-winning cyclists.

Tumi's Bicycle Club started with 10 members in 2008. Now we have 60. We want to spread the message to all Basotho and youth from outside the country too: if we work together, we can achieve anything.

That's why I was so happy when I got an e-mail from Stan and Nic. They'd seen my club website, and wanted to visit the club and see what we are doing here. They rode their bikes all the way from Cape Town with luggage and big cameras, and spent three days taking pictures. They were so excited to meet me – I was just as excited and I got a group of my club kids together to welcome them at the border. From Stan and Nic I've learnt that it's possible to get people interested in cycling by doing unique things.

When they left I rode with them out of Lesotho – it was a long way, but I wanted to show the respect I have for them. I wanted them to know what they came to Lesotho for. A lot of people know who I am here. It's nice to be known for doing good things, instead of for doing bad. I'm the bicycle guy.

Tumisang Taabe
President of Tumi's Bicycle Club, and deputy president
of the Lesotho Cycling Association

Mabusetsa Mpeete
Kingsway Road, Maseru, Lesotho
2011/05/03 15:13

'I constructed this bicycle in 2010 in one week. The design is something that came to me in a dream. I remember one Wednesday I thought about creating something. The next morning I woke up and went to buy materials, then I went back home and started making it. I'm not sure how much it cost to make. Ever since I constructed this bicycle, people have been staring at me and acknowledging my work, and giving me a pat on the back. It is good to have it because, firstly, I don't get sunburnt. Secondly, when it rains, I don't get wet. Thirdly, when I am travelling with my daughter, I take her on it. Fourthly, even when there are strong winds, I don't feel them. I have not finished it yet – I want to put in an engine. I don't have money now to buy the engine, but when I get it I will install it myself, without anyone's help. I will then put in the battery at the back, which will work with the engine and be charged by solar power.'

Ashston May
De Kock Street, Sunnyside, Pretoria, Gauteng, South Africa
2011/05/20 17:37

'Well, I have a wild history. There in the townships, you know how it goes. A man grows up with a hard life, you see, but I haven't lost focus. I may not have an education or anything, but my work keeps me going and I believe in God. I pray for my things. Here the people are saying that tomorrow's world is coming to an end – aaaah! The 21st, tomorrow is the 21st – here in the world, check my clock! Until that time, me, I just want to see what happens. From my experience, I mean, guys, get a life; come to your senses man. Just do right there, whatever you do – sin, pray. God forgives you 70 times 70 a day – not even the whole world can sin that much. I'm not trying to rhyme but my language is flowing. I can spit a little bit. But I can't freestyle cause my style ain't free – I just represent me. I heard I was streetwise, okay, so another *bra* showed me this place and I moved in with my roommate, and everything is *ńaa*, you see. We have a *ńaa* understanding and over-standing, we over-stand each other, you over-stand me? I'm a sales consultant at Sunglass Hut, I sell only original sunglasses. This is my best brand, Arnette. I won these glasses in a sales competition.

I don't take stuff, I work for my stuff. I don't steal stuff you see, look in my eyes, I work for my money. My dream is to make money, I want to get my things right, then one can look out for everybody who doesn't have. I have *tjommies* here in the street, I give them stuff that I didn't have. Don't underestimate the swag, I'm trying to be me. Like I said, I'm doing me. I have a tattoo of a tiger on my chest, representing my personality. *Eish*, I realised I needed to do something with my life, so I decided to move to another place. I got here and got myself a life, got a job. I'm trying to be famous, and I'm gonna do what you do to get my own. Word is, peace out everybody. Represent AKA Ashston! Word is playa! Over-stand this, call stout Ashstos, because I wised up. I know my game style, so I got to wise up. *Jy kan dit nie doen nie*, because I will tell you; shut up. *Ek is warm soos enige* setup, now you wanna check up 'cause my money went up, east up, east Sunnyside is where I'm at. *Son op jy is son af*. Love *en weer op met 'n* twist like twister but never rest, the disaster of the Ashstonishter. There is only one chance, if I don't make it I don't know. This one is for my baby…'

Bontle Moeng
Hill of Good Hope, Springfield Road, Midrand, Gauteng, South Africa
2011/04/28 19:38

'I entered a competition courtesy of Design Indaba. I saw on the website that they were giving away a Biomega NYC bicycle by KiBiSi. I'm sure NYC stands for New York City. I just tried my luck and entered. Basically they were looking for ideas on how to encourage cycling in South Africa. Most of the ideas I tweeted came straight from my head. The tweets included making a proposal to the National City Parks to install bicycle-friendly routes as part of public recreational activity, communicate the bicycle-to-work plan to South African citizens in all 11 official languages, and direct, produce and release a proudly South African bicycle-themed movie. This is the tweet that won: "Create a bicycle-ride brand identity with South African national colours and execute a proactive bicycle-to-work campaign using sports idols." I've never owned a bicycle, even in my childhood days. I'm hoping to be a professional cyclist in the next few months, ha ha! It will take a bit of work and a bit of time. I'm just excited about it. The first step would be to start riding around my complex. As soon as I'm comfortable and confident I'll try cycling to work. Most people can't believe I won the bicycle. My boyfriend is very supportive and is even willing to give up some of his free time to teach me. As soon as I'm ready I'll take off the wrappers and start riding, probably in the next few days…'

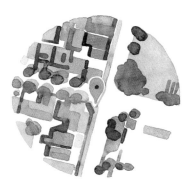

Kleinbooi Kabinde
Kirschner Road, Boksburg, Gauteng, South Africa
2011/06/28 15:12

'I make broomsticks. I am from KwaMhlanga in KwaNdebele and I am
from the Ndebele royal family. Now I am in Boksburg, working hard so
that my children will have something to eat. I got this bicycle from my
former boss, who felt compassion for me and gave it to me. I've had
it for four years. I have been here in Boksburg since 1961 – that's
when I started making broomsticks. I made the racks out of the
need to carry all my stock. I even made the carrier in front – for
the hand-held brooms known as *hand besems*.'

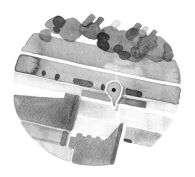

Victor Makhonofane
St Andrews Street, Bloemfontein, Free State, South Africa
2011/03/02 08:49

'This shop is called Loving Take Away and Heli Corner. They sell food, cold drinks and aeroplanes. I just make a few cents here because I don't have work. I've been here about a year and a half. I do deliveries – food, newspapers and cold drinks – but I've never delivered an aeroplane though. I've seen them flying next to the *Boeremark*. I don't have my own bicycle, but nothing is bad for me here, everything is good. I've only fallen once, the day I started working here. There was traffic; there were some people who didn't drive nicely. I got hurt, but not badly. So I just need to watch out. Originally I'm from a farm, where I grew up. Mr Johan Raath taught me how to cycle.'

Appie van der Merwe
R27, outside Calvinia, Northern Cape, South Africa
2011/04/13 14:54

'I cycled to Bloemfontein once – it's over 900 kilometres away. *Nou ja*, I bought a bicycle and once a week I cycled from the farm to Calvinia – for the exercise. Then one morning, I decided I was fit enough. I went to the headmaster of the school and said I want to raise some money for you, you should advertise. They went and organised some sponsorship per kilometre. To make a long story short, I cycled for five days, alone, just like that, from Calvinia to Bloemfontein. It was summer – there was rain, thunder, headwinds, with uphills and downhills, but I cycled in stages and did it easily. Then I felt alive. I was almost 50 then. When I gave up farming and moved to Calvinia I cycled almost every day, 10 kilometres out and then 10 kilometres back. But I got ill and ended up in hospital and didn't ride for a few months. So now I try to go every now and then – you know I'm almost 80 years old now! So if I feel good, like today, then I ride out as far as I can feel I can go, not overdoing it – I'm afraid of my heart stopping. I live in the old-age home now. I ride a bit, stop and look around at the world, and then I ride back. I also need to look at my watch, can't stay out too late – I'll get to the home and they'll have locked me out! Ha ha. Your biggest treasure that the Lord can give you on earth is your health. *Ou maat*, if you come to the stage I'm in and you get sick and need to lie in bed, you may have money, you may be able to pay the doctors, but money can't buy your health – that is something you need to look after yourself. My bicycle stands inside the old-age home, in the corridor. I push it through down the long corridor, and then through the dining room where the old people eat, out of the front door, then I go and ride.'

Mario Wetman
Commissioner Street, Boksburg, Gauteng, South Africa
2011/06/28 12:47

'I am from Mozambique. From 1981 I was fixing bicycles. Then I went
to work in the mines. After the mine was shut down, I came back to
my bicycle workshop. People bring their bicycles and I fix them. But
I am not making enough money, because there are not a lot of people
who cycle. And others, you fix their bicycle for them and then they
don't pay…'

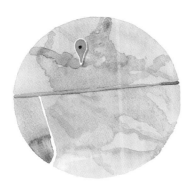

Mornay George
Off the R329, outside Steytlerville, Eastern Cape, South Africa
2010/08/12 19:07

'I'm visiting the area from Port Elizabeth. This morning I felt like
a bit of exercise… My old friend lives about 50 kilometres outside
of Steytlerville, on Bosfontein farm. I walked and jogged there this
morning and he lent me this bicycle to come back. After I'd been
cycling for about 20 kilometres, the right-hand pedal broke off.
So I've been walking for the last 30 kilometres. I mean, I enjoy
it – it's still part of my exercise. I'm not angry with the bicycle.'

Nkosilathi Mpofu
Helen Street, Buccleuch, Johannesburg, Gauteng, South Africa
2011/06/26 14:49

'I am on my way from work now; I'm going home to Tembisa. This is
my bicycle. I bought it from my boss for just R600. I use a bicycle all
the time. I prefer a bicycle because I can save money – taxi fares are
high! I don't earn much as a gardener. That is why I cycle Monday to
Sunday. With the little that I earn I can buy food for my children and
clothes for myself. This bicycle is from an old collection, from Italy.
But when there is a problem I can easily go and buy parts and
service it. I love this bike; it is like a child to me! If someone stole it,
they would break my heart. It is very strong, it is amazing. I use it
daily, from sunrise to sunset. In my backpack I have my cycling
shoes, clothes and food that was a gift from my boss. And there
are clothes that I used when I was in church – we had an all-night
prayer meeting yesterday.'

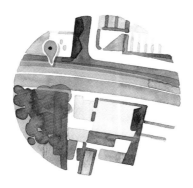

Lizette Chirrime
Victoria Road, Woodstock, Cape Town, Western Cape, South Africa
2010/06/12 11:24

'It's good for the environment and helps to keep things clean. It's also cheaper for me, because I don't have to pay for taxis. I don't get stuck in the traffic, you know, I just keep going. A taxi hit me once – the drivers don't respect me. They think, "How can you ride here?" but I just want to have a piece of street to ride in. I keep pushing; I believe I can make it. I've been riding for two years and I have survived. As a single mom with two children it is sometimes really tough to make ends meet. That is why the bicycle helps. Sometimes I take my boy to the crèche on the bicycle. I'm a visual artist, I paint and stitch. I make clothes and lamp shades, I recycle materials, all kinds of things…'

Atang Tshikare
Beach Road, Sea Point, Cape Town, Western Cape, South Africa
2011/03/05 18:38

'When I go to Bloemfontein, I borrow my grandmother's bicycle for all the things that I do. Legal and illegal – well, graffiti, that is. It is a long story. I used to do graffiti with a guy from Germany. Basically we once got caught doing graffiti with a bicycle. The odd thing was, because he was a white guy and I was a black guy, we got away with it. If we were both black or both white, we would have never got away with it. He gave my grandmother this bicycle. People who aren't South Africans often don't know how things used to happen, but we lived in a homeland called Bophuthatswana. In those days as a South African you weren't allowed to do many things. My grandmother used to work for some people doing house-cleaning work, and then she used to sell things in the streets, going to schools and selling food like *vetkoek*, *snoek* and things like that. She'd go to different schools. The nice thing about the bike was that she could take all her stuff and put it on the bike and travel from one place to another. Even when she was finished selling, she still used to go to church with her bicycle. I enjoy that I can go back and still borrow the same bike that she uses.

I can avoid a lot of people that I don't want to talk to and be inconspicuous, because a lot of people know me there. I was a radio DJ, I was doing graffiti and I had my own business. So every time I go back I try and avoid some people. If you're on a bicycle, people don't acknowledge you, even if you wear a suit – and that is perfect for me. If I can go around and not be seen, that is so much nicer. Day or night, it is perfect.'

Alfas Matonsela
Jan van Riebeeck Street, Ermelo, Mpumalanga, South Africa
2011/07/09 18:09

'It is very cold today. I've just come to the shop here. I'm on my way
home from work. I love this town, Ermelo – it's where I grew up. And
I love my bicycle. It was difficult when I had to walk everywhere, but
with the bicycle it's much easier to get around town. With this bicycle
everything is all right.'

Frans Pieterse
Victory Road, Greenside, Johannesburg, Gauteng, South Africa
2011/01/22 08:51

'Without the bicycle I wouldn't get through life. It takes me to work
and back, and basically puts food on the table. It is a little stressful
on the roads and one has to watch out for the cars, but I enjoy cycling
more than driving a car. I've had many accidents. Like a car driving in
front of me and then I fall over the bonnet, scratch my arms and break
a finger or so – but I just get back on the bicycle and cycle on. I can't
get along without my bicycle. I listen to RSG on my radio, it keeps me
company – you don't have anyone to chat to while you cycle. I've been
working at the same place for seven years. They are looking out for
me and treat me well, so I'm staying there. The bicycle's name is
Rainbow – since the early days she has been a she. I've been cycling
for 20 years now, since I was 14. I'm carrying some bones for my
dogs in here; there was a party at my work last night and I'm
taking the leftovers home.'

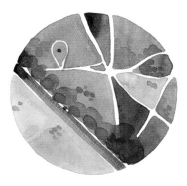

Boetie Meyer
Off the R43, outside Worcester, Western Cape, South Africa
2011/05/07 13:21

'I've been living in Worcester for 13 years. I grew up in Stellenbosch in the Western Cape. I've been a cyclist for seven years. I ride as much as 20, 30, 40 kilometres a day, to rugby practice and work. I work at a graphics company. We make vinyl signs to put on buses, wine tankers, trucks, bicycles, cars, ambulances – anything that needs a name or a sign. I really love my bicycle. This is my third one and it's a track bike. I must say that I have a problem with racing bicycles, I just don't like them. I always wanted one until I got a track bike. It inspires me to be a better rider. It's a privilege for for me to be able to ride my bicycle, I feel like I'm transported to another world when I'm riding. I prefer using the power from my body, mostly my legs, to control my bike. I've used a bike in the past that had brakes, but there can be problems, like the brake cable breaks, or a brake block sticks or jumps off. We are about seven or eight guys who ride track bikes. We like dicing each other, on the tar roads – there is no cycling track around here. We don't wear any protection because we feel that we are better off without protection because we know how to handle ourselves. The frame that I'm riding is from 1992, it's reasonably heavy, so when I'm riding against the wind it's like I'm riding two bicycles. I would spend a lot of money on my wheels, but there is nothing wrong with this frame. Looking to the future, it would be nice to have a lighter frame, but it would have to be only for racing. And I would have to be more careful with it – a light aluminium frame would not last, considering what I put the steel frames through.'

Advocate Ngwenya and **Jim Herps**
Eeufees Street, Bethal, KwaZulu-Natal, South Africa
2011/07/10 17:42

Advocate: 'My name is Advocate, my surname is Ngwenya. My surname means "crocodile". A crocodile lives underwater, but I do not live underwater – I live on the surface! And if you look at a crocodile it doesn't take a bath, although it lives underwater – but I do take a bath, ha ha! As you can see, I smell better anyway, ha ha! Yes, that is my surname, I don't like it. You shouldn't be scared of me… I live here in Bethal. I love my bike. It takes me everywhere I want to go, except when I have to go to far away places. I use it a lot because it saves me money. Unlike taking a taxi and using it to come to town. I usually use my bike.'

Jim: 'My name is Jim and my surname is Herps. I like my bike so very much. It can take me anywhere… Normally around here people use taxis, but my bike does not cost me anything. That is why I love it so much. So, I will stick with it.'

Hinrhic Onkers
Outside Blomnek, De Rust, Western Cape, South Africa
2010/05/12 16:34

'I'm busy building this bike. I got it from my big brother. He bought
himself a new one and he gave me this frame. This little red one
behind me used to be mine, but I handed it down to my little
brother. My father bought me that one, but he's passed away.
My brother gave me this silver one because I'm growing. It's got
a lot of aluminium parts. I need to buy some tubes and tyres for it
– I always buy slicks. Oh, and I need to get brake blocks. That's
why I'm not riding it yet – I still have some work to do on it. The front
wheel is locked in the storeroom. I was working on it and I saw that
the tube had burst. It's fucked up. That's dangerous to ride on – you'll
never be able to patch it.'

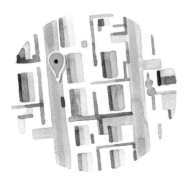

Koos Ruiters
Gravenor Street, Port Nolloth, Northern Cape, South Africa
2011/11/04 13:55

'A person doesn't normally know where to start … but, okay. I'm
Koos Ruiters. I've been living in Port Nolloth for the last 20 years.
I work as a security officer and everything I do there is very good
for me, and I love my work. I've always loved riding a bicycle. It
keeps a person healthy and it keeps your life stable. If this bike
had to be stolen it would be like a second life that leaves me… I've
had a car before, but my first priority has always been the bicycle
– because the price of fuel goes up and a bicycle doesn't use fuel.
You can zip into tight spots where cars can't go. So this is like my
bread and butter standing here next to me. I painted it like this but
it used to be a pale-golden colour. I ride it without brakes – this way
no other person can ride it; only I know how to handle it. I would
encourage people to fall in love with cycling. Sometimes people
don't feel like cycling because they have a car, they just want to
get there in comfort, but a bicycle is healthier. That is what I can
say about my bicycle.'

Madyna Mwoya
Persimmon Street, Malvern East, Germiston, Gauteng, South Africa
2011/06/28 10:43

'I never walk anywhere, because I prefer the bicycle. I thank the white people who gave me this bicycle – for the gift they gave me. I know how to ride this bicycle. The person who taught me how to ride is my husband. My home is very far from the shop where I work – that is why he taught me how to ride. The goodness of this bicycle is that it goes very fast, unlike the ones in the village in Malawi. At home I used to ride a bicycle nicely, and if there was a bad spot in the road I would stop, get off and then see where the road is good again and ride further. When I started riding I had an accident. I was riding one day on a downhill, I just went straight down without braking and fell straight into a drain. I was admitted to hospital because of that accident, but after the accident I improved, and I never had another accident. Now, no matter how long the distance, I ride it perfectly. The difference between the bicycles from home and the bicycle from here is that those ones from home need men to ride them – this one is much better, softer and more comfortable.'

Charles Khoza
Commissioner Street, Johannesburg, Gauteng, South Africa
2011/07/27 16:43

'My name is Charlie. This bicycle helps me a lot, because I sell safety products, like safety boots, dust coats and two-piece overalls. I just travel around on this bicycle, dropping goods to the workshops and other companies all over Jo'burg. That is how I feed my children and pay for their school, and put food on the plates at home. I chose this cruiser style over a mountain bike because I can ride nicely and sit up straight – and it's very comfortable. I don't get tired, I can just keep going. It's number one, this cruiser bicycle!'

Jackson Mithani
Voortrekker Street, Pofadder, Northern Cape, South Africa
2011/04/12 09:24

'I'm from Pofadder and I work at Ravanmar Garage. This is my work
bicycle. If I get sent to collect something in town or anywhere, I take
this bicycle. I also have my own bicycle – a mountain bike. I love it
and I'm very good on it. It comes from America, but I bought it here in
Pofadder for R1 500. It's so beautiful and light, and I can ride wherever
I want to. For the long road my Trek is number one! I want to compete
in races, but there aren't any around here. But I want to try. It's my life.
I've got my choice! Thank you!'

Joseph Mukubyne
Pienaar Street, Brooklyn, Pretoria, Gauteng, South Africa
2010/05/15 10:24

'I love cycling so much! I'm selling these oranges, one by one; I sell
them all over the place. I ask R1 an orange. There are only two bags
on here now, but I sell about four to seven bags on Saturdays. When
I sell them I'll have enough money to fix this tyre. I want to buy some
patch and solution at the Game store, and then I'll ride this bicycle
again. Yes, then I won't have problems. I'm from Hammanskraal but
live near Monument. I go all the way up there, ha ha, it's hard with one
gear, but I do it. I only bought the frame and then fixed it up. Some
of the parts had been thrown away and I found them at the dump.'

Themba Mbanga with Benjamin Morweng
Barkly Road, Homestead, Kimberley, Northern Cape, South Africa
2010/08/05 18:07

Themba: 'This is Uncle Bonyan's bicycle. He just borrowed it to
us to go buy petrol for the generator, so we can plug in the TV.
I don't have my own bicycle.'
Benjamin: 'I have my own bicycle, but we don't cycle to school.'
Themba: 'I like cycling because it is quicker to get to places.'

Alfred Ndamane
Drommedaris Road, Mbekweni, Wellington, Western Cape, South Africa
2011/05/06 17:42

'I live here in Mbekweni, in Project 2. I'm a bicycle user. The
bicycle always makes me get to work quickly and does not leave
me disappointed. I work long hours and after that I'm tired; I enjoy
cycling then. Nothing makes me angry; every day I go to church
and at weekends I stay with my brothers from church, and I have
a lot of friends. Everything I do is from my God, because I'm a child
of God. I was born again and I'm a new creation. I've painted my
bike this way, because when I'm on the road I want to be seen as a
Buccaneer from Orlando Pirates. So even though I'm a Kaizer Chiefs
fan, I want people to know where the Chiefs are from – they originated
from the Pirates, so the colours should look like the Pirates. Pirates
is the big team that birthed all the other teams. When you don't have
money for petrol, then you can go with your bicycle, even if you are
going far. Mine is a mountain bike. It has strength. I've had it for three
years and it is still strong, and working well without any trouble.'

Calvin Lechoba
James Scott Street, Thaba Nchu, Free State, South Africa
2011/03/03 18:31

'I went to Botshabelo, right, and came back. I went to Tweespruit,
then to Botshabelo and after that I went to Ditrust in Thaba Nchu.
I have gloves and a cap and also weights. I buy them for my bicycle.
You see these weights, I put them on when I go exercising. I like the
weights, because I need stamina. My bicycle is broken here at the
fork, and my brakes are broken, so I hope someone will be able
to help me fix it. *Ja,* it's like that.'

Simon Swartz
Stokroos Street, Campbell, Northern Cape, South Africa
2010/08/09 18:24

'My bicycle is my legs. I use it to pick up wood – anything. I've been riding for a long time, since I was small. I'm 63 now – it's my life. I'll ride to Kimberley, to Douglas, in my own time. When I feel I need rest, I stop and I drink a little water. Then I get my breath again. The bicycle means so much to me. There are some people who cycle here in Campbell, but most people are not interested. You know if you are a loafer, you'll be a loafer on a bicycle too! I take care when I ride. When a car comes I pull over and I let it pass, then I go again. I don't see anything bad about a bicycle. It can't do anything to me, it gives me more power. I'm an old man, but it gives me the desire to run. I'm not tired. The bicycle keeps you alive – you just need to understand it and you need to know how hard you can ride. You can feel it in your legs.'

Sipho Malhobo
16th Avenue, Alexandra, Johannesburg, Gauteng, South Africa
2011/06/26 16:41

'I stay in Alexandra. I'm going to tell you about my bicycle that was
stolen yesterday, but I don't feel good about it, because when you
like your things … that bike was new. I was going to Randburg and
then they stole it. I came home on my feet. But I'll buy another one.
I was very worried, because I work with it, I buy groceries with it,
when it is there I can make money with it. I can do a lot of things
with it. There are places that the taxis don't reach, but with the
bicycle I can get there. This one is the bicycle of my older brother.
So I'm going to fix up this one. If you want something, if you like it,
then you will go for it, because it's like a dream. And you won't give
up. You go for it, and you will be prosperous with it. *Ja*. Normally,
I cycle to my job or when I want to rush somewhere. With the bicycle
I can go there easily. There are so many things I want to do in life, *ja*.'

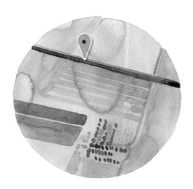

Mickey Mampe
R64, outside Dealesville, Free State, South Africa
2011/03/01 08:10

'The men are happy when I'm on a bicycle. We can go anywhere because we know how to ride bicycles. It helps nicely, you don't struggle, you just get on it. I'm going from here to Daniel Jacobs' farm to charge my phone, and then I want to get a bicycle with thin wheels to go to another farm. I would like to have a thin-wheeled racer bike to go to Boshof to visit my mom. I don't like a horse cart, it hurts. When you climb on, it's bumpy, but when you are on a bicycle it is nice. You just ride, and if it gets a puncture you patch it, and then you can go.'

Graphic designer **Gabrielle Guy** and artist **Gabrielle Raaff** might share the same first name (which resulted in quite a few misdirected e-mails during the course of this project), but that's where the similarity between these two Capetonians ends. Gaby Guy loves making art books and taking afternoon naps. She currently owns a cheap '80s pink-and-white ladies' racer that she partly restored herself, although she hopes to upgrade to something cooler soon. Gabby Raaff (with an extra 'b') enjoys painting South African people and their neighbourhoods in watercolour from oblique angles, often using satellite imagery. Her bike was stolen a while ago and she is currently in the market for a well-travelled replacement.

This project would not have been possible without the support of Xander Smith, Hilton Tennant, Gary King, Brad Quartuccio, Guy Pearce, Henta and Dareen Engelbrecht, Nic and Sonia Grobler, Nora Swart, Roger and Elca Grobler, Olympic Cycles, Darrel Wratten, Johan Kotze, Henning Rasmuss, Louis de Waal, Simon Barlow, Christine Campbell, Ivin Greyling, Gordon Roy, Jean-Pierre Nortier, Joan Morgenstern, Mervyn Leong, Howard Pulchin, Owen Clipsham, Martin Palmer, Richard Bingham, Conrad Dempsey, Doug Ingram, Peter Newbury and Jörg Diekmann.

Published by Day One, 2012 / www.dayone.co.za / ISBN 978-0-620-52253-3

Design and layout Gabrielle Guy
Illustrations Gabrielle Raaff
Illustration assistance Allan and Jenny Raaff
Additional text Karen Robertson, Sean Wilson
Copy editing Deborah Louw, Ania Rokita
Translations Bolekwa Sesmani, Selloane Khalane, Atang Tshikare, Judy Brandao
Printing Tien Wah Press, Singapore

When **Stan Engelbrecht** and **Nic Grobler** initiated this project, they aimed for it to be a study of South African bicycle commuter culture. They wanted to find out who rides bicycles, why they ride them, if and why they love them, and of course why so few South Africans choose the bicycle as an alternative means of transport.

Stan's fascination with the mechanics of the bicycle and his background in photography, and Nic's interest in the role the bicycle plays in a community, brought them together to collaborate on a bicycle-related project. They imagined finding classic '70s Italian-built racers that had become hand-me-down commuter bikes, and photographing their weathered riders.

What started as a short ride around the area where they both live became a 6 000 kilometre journey over two years, taking them clear across the country. They traversed the Maluti mountains, sweated through Durban's humid climes, braved the blustery West Coast winds, got sunburnt outside Addo, and built up trashed bicycles in Maputo and rode them back to Johannesburg. They cycled everywhere to meet the bold individuals photographed for this project – people who choose to ride a bicycle in the face of cultural and social stigma, crime and dangerous roads.

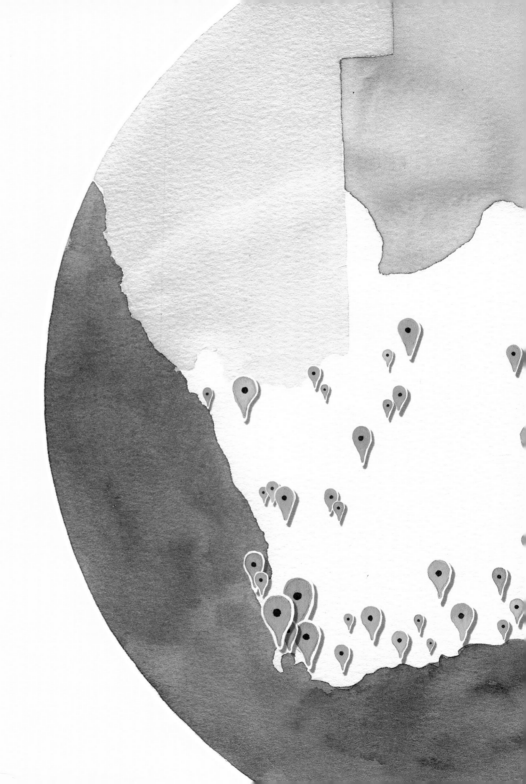